ENDYMION.

A Romance.

Printed by T. Miller, Noble street, Cheapside

ENDYMION:

A Poetic Romance.

BY JOHN KEATS

"THE STRETCHED METRE OF AN ANTIQUE SONG"

LONDON

PRINTED FOR TAYLOR AND HESSEY,

93, FLEET STREET

1818

INSCRIBED

TO THE MEMORY

OF

THOMAS CHATTERTON

PREFACE

KNOWING within myself the manner in which this Poem has been produced, it is not without a feeling of regret that I make it public

What manner I mean, will be quite clear to the reader, who must soon perceive great inexperience, immaturity, and every error denoting a feverish attempt, rather than a deed accomplished The two first books, and indeed the two last, I feel sensible are not of such completion as to warrant their passing the press, nor should they if I thought a year's castigation would do them any good ,—it will not · the foundations are too sandy. It is just that this youngster should die away a sad thought for me, if I had not some hope that while it is dwindling I may be plotting, and fitting myself for verses fit to live

This may be speaking too presumptuously, and may deserve a punishment but no feeling man will be forward to inflict it he will leave me alone, with the conviction that there is not a fiercer hell than the failure in a great object. This is not written with the least atom of purpose to forestall criticisms of course, but from the desire I have to conciliate men who are competent to look, and who do look with a zealous eye, to the honour of English literature.

The imagination of a boy is healthy, and the mature imagination of a man is healthy, but there is a space of life between, in which the soul is in a ferment, the character undecided, the way of life uncertain, the ambition thick-sighted: thence proceeds mawkishness, and all the thousand bitters which those men I speak of must necessarily taste in going over the following pages

I hope I have not in too late a day touched the beautiful mythology of Greece, and dulled its brightness. for I wish to try once more, before I bid it farewel.

Teignmouth,
April 10, 1818

ERRATUM

Page 108, line 4 from the bottom, for " her" read " his "

ENDYMION.

BOOK I

ENDYMION.

BOOK I.

A THING of beauty is a joy for ever
Its loveliness increases, it will never
Pass into nothingness, but still will keep
A bower quiet for us, and a sleep
Full of sweet dreams, and health, and quiet breathing.
Therefore, on every morrow, are we wreathing
A flowery band to bind us to the earth,
Spite of despondence, of the inhuman dearth
Of noble natures, of the gloomy days,
Of all the unhealthy and o'er-darkened ways   10

Made for our searching   yes, in spite of all,
Some shape of beauty moves away the pall
From our dark spirits. Such the sun, the moon,
Trees old and young, sprouting a shady boon
For simple sheep, and such are daffodils
With the green world they live in, and clear rills
That for themselves a cooling covert make
'Gainst the hot season, the mid forest brake,
Rich with a sprinkling of fair musk-rose blooms
And such too is the grandeur of the dooms   2(
We have imagined for the mighty dead,
All lovely tales that we have heard or read
An endless fountain of immortal drink,
Pouring unto us from the heaven's brink

    Nor do we merely feel these essences
For one short hour, no, even as the trees
That whisper round a temple become soon
Dear as the temple's self, so does the moon,
The passion poesy, glories infinite,
Haunt us till they become a cheering light   '
Unto our souls, and bound to us so fast,

That, whether there be shine, or gloom o'ercast,
They alway must be with us, or we die.

Therefore, 'tis with full happiness that I
Will trace the story of Endymion.
The very music of the name has gone
Into my being, and each pleasant scene
Is growing fresh before me as the green
Of our own vallies   so I will begin
Now while I cannot hear the city's din,   40
Now while the early budders are just new,
And run in mazes of the youngest hue
About old forests, while the willow trails
Its delicate amber, and the dairy pails
Bring home increase of milk   And, as the year
Grows lush in juicy stalks, I'll smoothly steer
My little boat, for many quiet hours,
With streams that deepen freshly into bowers
Many and many a verse I hope to write,
Before the daisies, vermeil rimm'd and white,   50
Hide in deep herbage, and ere yet the bees
Hum about globes of clover and sweet peas,

I must be near the middle of my story
O may no wintry season, bare and hoary,
See it half finished . but let Autumn bold,
With universal tinge of sober gold,
Be all about me when I make an end
And now at once, adventuresome, I send
My herald thought into a wilderness
There let its trumpet blow, and quickly dress   60
My uncertain path with green, that I may speed
Easily onward, thorough flowers and weed

    Upon the sides of Latmos was outspread
A mighty forest, for the moist earth fed
So plenteously all weed-hidden roots
Into o'er-hanging boughs, and precious fruits
And it had gloomy shades, sequestered deep,
Where no man went, and if from shepherd's keep
A lamb strayed far a-down those inmost glens,
Never again saw he the happy pens   70
Whither his brethren, bleating with content,
Over the hills at every nightfall went
Among the shepherds, 'twas believed ever,

That not one fleecy lamb which thus did sever

From the white flock, but pass'd unworried

By angry wolf, or pard with prying head,

Until it came to some unfooted plains

Where fed the herds of Pan   ay great his gains

Who thus one lamb did lose   Paths there were many,

Winding through palmy fern, and rushes fenny,   80

And ivy banks, all leading pleasantly

To a wide lawn, whence one could only see

Stems thronging all around between the swel¹

Of turf and slanting branches   who could tell

The freshness of the space of heaven above,

Edg'd round with dark tree tops ? through which a dove

Would often 'reat its wings, and often too

A little cloud would move across the blue

Full in the middle of this pleasantness

There stood a marble altar, with a tress   90

Of flowers budded newly, and the dew

Had taken fairy phantasies to strew

Daisies upon the sacred sward last eve,

And so the dawned light in pomp receive.

For 'twas the morn   Apollo's upward fire
Made every eastern cloud a silvery pyre
Of brightness so unsullied, that therein
A melancholy spirit well might win
Oblivion, and melt out his essence fine
Into the winds   rain-scented eglantine   100
Gave temperate sweets to that well-wooing sun ,
The lark was lost in him , cold springs had run
To warm their chilliest bubbles in the grass ,
Man's voice was on the mountains , and the mass
Of nature's lives and wonders puls'd tenfold,
To feel this sun-rise and its glories old

Now while the silent workings of the dawn
Were busiest, into that self-same lawn
All suddenly, with joyful cries, there sped
A troop of little children garlanded,   11(
Who gathering round the altar, seemed to pry
Earnestly round as wishing to espy
Some folk of holiday   nor had they waited
For many moments, ere their ears were sated
With a faint breath of music, which ev'n then

Fill'd out its voice, and died away again
Within a little space again it gave
Its airy swellings, with a gentle wave,
To light-hung leaves, in smoothest echoes breaking
Through copse-clad vallies,—ere their death, o'ertaking
The surgy murmurs of the lonely sea.   121

And now, as deep into the wood as we
Might mark a lynx's eye, there glimmered light
Fair faces and a rush of garments white,
Plainer and plainer shewing, till at last
Into the widest alley they all past,
Making directly for the woodland altar.
O kindly muse! let not my weak tongue faulter
In telling of this goodly company,
Of their old piety, and of their glee   130
But let a portion of ethereal dew
Fall on my head, and presently unmew
My soul, that I may dare, in wayfaring,
To stammer where old Chaucer used to sing

Leading the way, young damsels danced along,

Bearing the burden of a shepherd song,

Each having a white wicker over brimm'd

With April's tender younglings next, well trimm'd,

A crowd of shepherds with as sunburnt looks

As may be read of in Arcadian books,   140

Such as sat listening round Apollo's pipe,

When the great deity, for earth too ripe,

Let his divinity o'er-flowing die

In music, through the vales of Thessaly

Some idly trailed their sheep-hooks on the ground,

And some kept up a shrilly mellow sound

With ebon-tipped flutes close after these,

Now coming from beneath the forest trees,

A venerable priest full soberly,

Begirt with ministring looks alway his eye   150

Stedfast upon the matted turf he kept,

And after him his sacred vestments swept

From his right hand there swung a vase, milk-white,

Of mingled wine, out-sparkling generous light,

And in his left he held a basket full

Of all sweet herbs that searching eye could cull

Wild thyme, and valley-lilies whiter still

Than Leda's love, and cresses from the rill
His aged head, crowned with beechen wreath,
Seem'd like a poll of ivy in the teeth   160
Of winter hoar   Then came another crowd
Of shepherds, lifting in due time aloud
Their share of the ditty   After them appear'd,
Up-followed by a multitude that rear'd
Their voices to the clouds, a fair wrought car,
Easily rolling so as scarce to mar
The freedom of three steeds of dapple brown
Who stood therein did seem of great renown
Among the throng   His youth was fully blown,
Shewing like Ganymede to manhood grown,   170
And, for those simple times, his garments were
A chieftain king's   beneath his breast, half bare,
Was hung a silver bugle, and between
His nervy knees there lay a boar-spear keen
A smile was on his countenance, he seem'd,
To common lookers on, like one who dream'd
Of idleness in groves Elysian
But there were some who feelingly could scan
A lurking trouble in his nether lip,

And see that oftentimes the reins would slip   180
Through his forgotten hands   then would they sigh,
And think of yellow leaves, of owlets cry,
Of logs piled solemnly.—Ah, well-a-day,
Why should our young Endymion pine away!

    Soon the assembly, in a circle rang'd,
Stood silent round the shrine   each look was chang'd
To sudden veneration   women meek
Beckon'd their sons to silence, while each cheek
Of virgin bloom paled gently for slight fear
Endymion too, without a forest peer,   190
Stood, wan, and pale, and with an awed face,
Among his brothers of the mountain chase.
In midst of all, the venerable priest
Eyed them with joy from greatest to the least,
And, after lifting up his aged hands,
Thus spake he   " Men of Latmos! shepherd bands!
Whose care it is to guard a thousand flocks
Whether descended from beneath the rocks
That overtop your mountains, whether come
From vallies where the pipe is never dumb,   200

Or from your swelling downs, where sweet air stirs

Blue hare-bells lightly, and where prickly furze

Buds lavish gold, or ye, whose precious charge

Nibble their fill at ocean's very marge,

Whose mellow reeds are touch'd with sounds forlorn

By the dim echoes of old Triton's horn

Mothers and wives! who day by day prepare

The scrip, with needments. for the mountain air,

And all ye gentle girls who foster up

Udderless lambs, and in a little cup   210

Will put choice honey for a favoured youth

Yea, every one attend! for in good truth

Our vows are wanting to our great god Pan

Are not our lowing heifers sleeker than

Night-swollen mushrooms? Are not our wide plains

Speckled with countless fleeces? Have not rains

Green'd over April's lap? No howling sad

Sickens our fearful ewes, and we have had

Great bounty from Endymion our lord

The earth is glad the merry lark has pour'd   220

His early song against yon breezy sky,

That spreads so clear o'er our solemnity "

Thus ending, on the shrine he heap'd a spire

Of teeming sweets, enkindling sacred fire,

Anon he stain'd the thick and spongy sod

With wine, in honour of the shepherd-god

Now while the earth was drinking it, and while

Bay leaves were crackling in the fragrant pile,

And gummy frankincense was sparkling bright

'Neath smothering parsley, and a hazy light   230

Spread greyly eastward, thus a chorus sang

" O THOU, whose mighty palace roof doth hang

From jagged trunks, and overshadoweth

Eternal whispers, glooms, the birth, life, death

Of unseen flowers in heavy peacefulness,

Who lov'st to see the hamadryads dress

Their ruffled locks where meeting hazels darken,

And through whole solemn hours dost sit, and hearken

The dreary melody of bedded reeds—

In desolate places, where dank moisture breeds   240

The pipy hemlock to strange overgrowth,

Bethinking thee, how melancholy loth

Thou wast to lose fair Syrinx—do thou now,

By thy love's milky brow!

By all the trembling mazes that she ran,

Hear us, great Pan!

    " O thou, for whose soul-soothing quiet, turtles

Passion their voices cooingly 'mong myrtles,

What time thou wanderest at eventide

Through sunny meadows, that outskirt the side   250

Of thine enmossed realms   O thou, to whom

Broad leaved fig trees even now foredoom

Their ripen'd fruitage, yellow girted bees

Their golden honeycombs, our village leas

Their fairest blossom'd beans and poppied corn,

The chuckling linnet its five young unborn,

To sing for thee, low creeping strawberries

Their summer coolness, pent up butterflies

Their freckled wings, yea, the fresh budding year

All its completions—be quickly near,   260

By every wind that nods the mountain pine,

O forester divine!

" Thou, to whom every fawn and satyr flies

For willing service, whether to surprise

The squatted hare while in half sleeping fit,

Or upward ragged precipices flit

To save poor lambkins from the eagle's maw,

Or by mysterious enticement draw

Bewildered shepherds to their path again,

Or to tread breathless round the frothy main,   270

And gather up all fancifullest shells

For thee to tumble into Naiads' cells,

And, being hidden, laugh at their out-peeping,

Or to delight thee with fantastic leaping,

The while they pelt each other on the crown

With silvery oak apples, and fir cones brown—

By all the echoes that about thee ring,

Hear us, O satyr king!

" O Hearkener to the loud clapping shears,

While ever and anon to his shorn peers   280

A ram goes bleating   Winder of the horn,

When snouted wild-boars routing tender corn

Anger our huntsman   Breather round our farms,

To keep off mildews, and all weather harms
Strange ministrant of undescribed sounds,
That come a swooning over hollow grounds,
And wither drearily on barren moors
Dread opener of the mysterious doors
Leading to universal knowledge—see,
Great son of Dryope,   290
The many that are come to pay their vows
With leaves about their brows !

     Be still the unimaginable lodge
For solitary thinkings , such as dodge
Conception to the very bourne of heaven,
Then leave the naked brain . be still the leaven,
That spreading in this dull and clodded earth
Gives it a touch ethereal—a new birth
Be still a symbol of immensity ,
A firmament reflected in a sea ,   300
An element filling the space between ,
An unknown—but no more   we humbly screen
With uplift hands our foreheads, lowly bending,
And giving out a shout most heaven rending,

                           c

Conjure thee to receive our humble Pæan,
Upon thy Mount Lycean!

Even while they brought the burden to a close,
A shout from the whole multitude arose,
That lingered in the air like dying rolls
Of abrupt thunder, when Ionian shoals   310
Of dolphins bob their noses through the brine
Meantime, on shady levels, mossy fine,
Young companies nimbly began dancing
To the swift treble pipe, and humming string
Aye, those fair living forms swam heavenly
To tunes forgotten—out of memory
Fair creatures! whose young childrens' children bred
Thermopylæ its heroes—not yet dead,
But in old marbles ever beautiful.
High genitors, unconscious did they cull   320
Time's sweet first-fruits—they danc'd to weariness,
And then in quiet circles did they press
The hillock turf, and caught the latter end
Of some strange history, potent to send

A young mind from its bodily tenement.

Or they might watch the quoit-pitchers, intent

On either side, pitying the sad death

Of Hyacinthus, when the cruel breath

Of Zephyr slew him,—Zephyr penitent,

Who now, ere Phœbus mounts the firmament,   330

Fondles the flower amid the sobbing rain

The archers too, upon a wider plain,

Beside the feathery whizzing of the shaft,

And the dull twanging bowstring, and the raft

Branch down sweeping from a tall ash top,

Call'd up a thousand thoughts to envelope

Those who would watch   Perhaps, the trembling knee

And frantic gape of lonely Niobe,

Poor, lonely Niobe ! when her lovely young

Were dead and gone, and her caressing tongue   340

Lay a lost thing upon her paly lip,

And very, very deadliness did nip

Her motherly cheeks.   Arous'd from this sad mood

By one, who at a distance loud halloo'd,

Uplifting his strong bow into the air,

Many might after brighter visions stare

After the Argonauts, in blind amaze

Tossing about on Neptune's restless ways,

Until, from the horizon's vaulted side,

There shot a golden splendour far and wide,   350

Spangling those million poutings of the brine

With quivering ore   'twas even an awful shine

From the exaltation of Apollo's bow,

A heavenly beacon in their dreary woe

Who thus were ripe for high contemplating,

Might turn their steps towards the sober ring

Where sat Endymion and the aged priest

'Mong shepherds gone in eld, whose looks increas'd

The silvery setting of their mortal star

There they discours'd upon the fragile bar   360

That keeps us from our homes ethereal,

And what our duties there   to nightly call

Vesper, the beauty-crest of summer weather,

To summon all the downiest clouds together

For the sun's purple couch, to emulate

In ministring the potent rule of fate

With speed of fire-tailed exhalations,

To tint her pallid cheek with bloom, who cons

Sweet poesy by moonlight   besides these,

A world of other unguess'd offices   370

Anon they wander'd, by divine converse,

Into Elysium, vieing to rehearse

Each one his own anticipated bliss

One felt heart-certain that he could not miss

His quick gone love, among fair blossom'd boughs,

Where every zephyr-sigh pouts, and endows

Her lips with music for the welcoming

Another wish'd, mid that eternal spring,

To meet his rosy child, with feathery sails,

Sweeping, eve-earnestly, through almond vales   380

Who, suddenly, should stoop through the smooth wind,

And with the balmiest leaves his temples bind,

And, ever after, through those regions be

His messenger, his little Mercury

Some were athirst in soul to see again

Their fellow huntsmen o'er the wide champaign

In times long past, to sit with them, and talk

Of all the chances in their earthly walk,

Comparing, joyfully, their plenteous stores

Of happiness, to when upon the moors,   390

Benighted, close they huddled from the cold,

And shar'd their famish'd scrips.   Thus all out-told

Their fond imaginations,—saving him

Whose eyelids curtain'd up their jewels dim,

Endymion. yet hourly had he striven

To hide the cankering venom, that had riven

His fainting recollections   Now indeed

His senses had swoon'd off · he did not heed

The sudden silence, or the whispers low,

Or the old eyes dissolving at his woe,   400

Or anxious calls, or close of trembling palms,

Or maiden's sigh, that grief itself embalms

But in the self-same fixed trance he kept,

Like one who on the earth had never stept.

Aye, even as dead-still as a marble man,

Frozen in that old tale Arabian.

Who whispers him so pantingly and close?

Peona, his sweet sister   of all those,

His friends, the dearest.   Hushing signs she made,

And breath'd a sister's sorrow to persuade   410

A yielding up, a cradling on her care.

Her eloquence did breathe away the curse·
She led him, like some midnight spirit nurse
Of happy changes in emphatic dreams,
Along a path between two little streams,—
Guarding his forehead, with her round elbow,
From low-grown branches, and his footsteps slow
From stumbling over stumps and hillocks small,
Until they came to where these streamlets fall,
With mingled bubblings and a gentle rush,   420
Into a river, clear, brimful, and flush
With crystal mocking of the trees and sky
A little shallop, floating there hard by,
Pointed its beak over the fringed bank,
And soon it lightly dipt, and rose, and sank,
And dipt again, with the young couple's weight,—
Peona guiding, through the water straight,
Towards a bowery island opposite,
Which gaining presently, she steered light
Into a shady, fresh, and ripply cove,   430
Where nested was an arbour, overwove
By many a summer's silent fingering,
To whose cool bosom she was used to bring

Her playmates, with their needle broidery,
And minstrel memories of times gone by

   So she was gently glad to see him laid
Under her favourite bower's quiet shade,
On her own couch, new made of flower leaves,
Dried carefully on the cooler side of sheaves
When last the sun his autumn tresses shook,   440
And the tann'd harvesters rich armfuls took
Soon was he quieted to slumbrous rest
But, ere it crept upon him, he had prest
Peona's busy hand against his lips,
And still, a sleeping, held her finger-tips
In tender pressure　And as a willow keeps
A patient watch over the stream that creeps
Windingly by it, so the quiet maid
Held her in peace　so that a whispering blade
Of grass, a wailful gnat, a bee bustling   450
Down in the blue-bells, or a wren light rustling
Among sere leaves and twigs, might all be heard.

   O magic sleep! O comfortable bird,

That broodest o'er the troubled sea of the mind

Till it is hush'd and smooth ! O unconfin'd

Restraint ! imprisoned liberty ! great key

To golden palaces, strange minstrelsy,

Fountains grotesque, new trees, bespangled caves,

Echoing grottos, full of tumbling waves

And moonlight, aye, to all the mazy world   460

Of silvery enchantment !—who, upfurl'd

Beneath thy drowsy wing a triple hour,

But renovates and lives?—Thus, in the bower,

Endymion was calm'd to life again

Opening his eyelids with a healthier brain,

He said   " I feel this thine endearing love

All through my bosom   thou art as a dove

Trembling its closed eyes and sleeked wings

About me, and the pearliest dew not brings

Such morning incense from the fields of May,   470

As do those brighter drops that twinkling stray

From those kind eyes,—the very home and haunt

Of sisterly affection   Can I want

Aught else, aught nearer heaven, than such tears?

Yet dry them up, in bidding hence all fears

That, any longer, I will pass my days
Alone and sad. No, I will once more raise
My voice upon the mountain-heights, once more
Make my horn parley from their foreheads hoar
Again my trooping hounds their tongues shall loll   480
Around the breathed boar. again I'll poll
The fair-grown yew tree, for a chosen bow.
And, when the pleasant sun is getting low,
Again I'll linger in a sloping mead
To hear the speckled thrushes, and see feed
Our idle sheep   So be thou cheered sweet,
And, if thy lute is here, softly intreat
My soul to keep in its resolved course."

    Hereat Peona, in their silver source,
Shut her pure sorrow drops with glad exclaim,   490
And took a lute, from which there pulsing came
A lively prelude, fashioning the way
In which her voice should wander. 'Twas a lay
More subtle cadenced, more forest wild
Than Dryope's lone lulling of her child,
And nothing since has floated in the air

So mournful strange. Surely some influence rare
Went, spiritual, through the damsel's hand;
For still, with Delphic emphasis, she spann'd
The quick invisible strings, even though she saw   500
Endymion's spirit melt away and thaw
Before the deep intoxication
But soon she came, with sudden burst, upon
Her self-possession—swung the lute aside,
And earnestly said " Brother, 'tis vain to hide
That thou dost know of things mysterious,
Immortal, starry , such alone could thus
Weigh down thy nature   Hast thou sinn'd in aught
Offensive to the heavenly powers? Caught
A Paphian dove upon a message sent?   510
Thy deathful bow against some deer-herd bent,
Sacred to Dian? Haply, thou hast seen
Her naked limbs among the alders green ,
And that, alas ' is death   No, I can trace
Something more high perplexing in thy face '"

Endymion look'd at her, and press'd her hand,
And said, " Art thou so pale, who wast so bland

And merry in our meadows? How is this?

Tell me thine ailment   tell me all amiss ! —

Ah ! thou hast been unhappy at the change   520

Wrought suddenly in me   What indeed more strange?

Or more complete to overwhelm surmise?

Ambition is no sluggard   'tis no prize,

That toiling years would put within my grasp,

That I have sigh'd for   with so deadly gasp

No man e'er panted for a mortal love

So all have set my heavier grief above

These things which happen   Rightly have they done

I, who still saw the horizontal sun

Heave his broad shoulder o'er the edge of the world, 530

Out-facing Lucifer, and then had hurl'd

My spear aloft, as signal for the chace—

I, who, for very sport of heart, would race

With my own steed from Araby , pluck down

A vulture from his towery perching , frown

A lion into growling, loth retire—

To lose, at once, all my toil breeding fire,

And sink thus low ! but I will ease my breast

Of secret grief, here in this bowery nest.

" This river does not see the naked sky,   540

Till it begins to progress silverly

Around the western border of the wood,

Whence, from a certain spot, its winding flood

Seems at the distance like a crescent moon

And in that nook, the very pride of June,

Had I been used to pass my weary eves ,

The rather for the sun unwilling leaves

So dear a picture of his sovereign power,

And I could witness his most kingly hour,

When he doth lighten up the golden reins,   550

And paces leisurely down amber plains

His snorting four   Now when his chariot last

Its beams against the zodiac-lion cast,

There blossom'd suddenly a magic bed

Of sacred ditamy, and poppies red

At which I wondered greatly, knowing well

That but one night had wrought this flowery spell ,

And, sitting down close by, began to muse

What it might mean. Perhaps, thought I, Morpheus,

In passing here, his owlet pinions shook ,   560

Or, it may be, ere matron Night uptook

Her ebon urn, young Mercury, by stealth,

Had dipt his rod in it   such garland wealth

Came not by common growth   Thus on I thought,

Until my head was dizzy and distraught

Moreover, through the dancing poppies stole

A breeze, most softly lulling to my soul,

And shaping visions all about my sight

Of colours, wings, and bursts of spangly light,

The which became more strange, and strange, and dim,

And tnen were gulph'd in a tumultuous swim   571

And then I fell asleep   Ah, can I tell

The enchantment that afterwards befel ?

Yet it was but a dream   yet such a dream

That never tongue, although it overteem

With mellow utterance, like a cavern spring,

Could figure out and to conception bring

All I beheld and felt.   Methought I lay

Watching the zenith, where the milky way

Among the stars in virgin splendour pours ,   580

And travelling my eye, until the doors

Of heaven appear'd to open for my flight,

I became loth and fearful to alight

From such high soaring by a downward glance ·

So kept me stedfast in that airy trance,

Spreading imaginary pinions wide

When, presently, the stars began to glide,

And faint away, before my eager view

At which I sigh'd that I could not pursue,

And dropt my vision to the horizon's verge,   590

And lo! from opening clouds, I saw emerge

The loveliest moon, that ever silver'd o'er

A shell for Neptune's goblet   she did soar

So passionately bright, my dazzled soul

Commingling with her argent spheres did roll

Through clear and cloudy, even when she went

At last into a dark and vapoury tent—

Whereat, methought, the lidless-eyed train

Of planets all were in the blue again

To commune with those orbs, once more I rais'd   600

My sight right upward   but it was quite dazed

By a bright something, sailing down apace,

Making me quickly veil my eyes and face

Again I look'd, and, O ye deities,

Who from Olympus watch our destinies !

Whence that completed form of all completeness ?

Whence came that high perfection of all sweetness ?

Speak, stubborn earth, and tell me where, O where

Hast thou a symbol of her golden hair ?

Not oat-sheaves drooping in the western sun ,   610

Not—thy soft hand, fair sister ! let me shun

Such follying before thee—yet she had,

Indeed, locks bright enough to make me mad ,

And they were simply gordian'd up and braided,

Leaving, in naked comeliness, unshaded,

Her pearl round ears, white neck, and orbed brow ,

The which were blended in, I know not how,

With such a paradise of lips and eyes,

Blush-tinted cheeks, half smiles, and faintest sighs,

That, when I think thereon, my spirit clings   620

And plays about its fancy, till the stings

Of human neighbourhood envenom all

Unto what awful power shall I call ?

To what high fane ?—Ah ! see her hovering feet,

More bluely vein'd, more soft, more whitely sweet

Than those of sea-born Venus, when she rose

From out her cradle shell   The wind out-blows

Her scarf into a fluttering pavilion,

'Tis blue, and over-spangled with a million

Of little eyes, as though thou wert to shed,   630

Over the darkest, lushest blue-bell bed,

Handfuls of daisies "—" Endymion, how strange !

Dream within dream !"—" She took an airy range,

And then, towards me, like a very maid,

Came blushing, waning, willing, and afraid,

And press'd me by the hand Ah ! 'twas too much,

Methought I fainted at the charmed touch,

Yet held my recollection, even as one

Who dives three fathoms where the waters run

Gurgling in beds of coral for anon,   640

I felt upmounted in that region

Where falling stars dart their artillery forth,

And eagles struggle with the buffeting north

That balances the heavy meteor-stone,—

Felt too, I was not fearful, nor alone,

But lapp'd and lull'd along the dangerous sky

Soon, as it seem'd, we left our journeying high,

And straightway into frightful eddies swoop'd,

Such as ay muster where grey time has scoop'd

D

Huge dens and caverns in a mountain's side   650

There hollow sounds arous'd me, and I sigh'd

To faint once more by looking on my bliss—

I was distracted, madly did I kiss

The wooing arms which held me, and did give

My eyes at once to death   but 'twas to live,

To take in draughts of life from the gold fount

Of kind and passionate looks, to count, and count

The moments, by some greedy help that seem'd

A second self, that each might be redeem'd

And plunder'd of its load of blessedness   660

Ah, desperate mortal ! I ev'n dar'd to press

Her very cheek against my crowned lip,

And, at that moment, felt my body dip

Into a warmer air   a moment more,

Our feet were soft in flowers   There was store

Of newest joys upon that alp   Sometimes

A scent of violets, and blossoming limes,

Loiter'd around us , then of honey cells,

Made delicate from all white-flower bells,

And once, above the edges of our nest,   670

An arch face peep'd,—an Oread as I guess'd

" Why did I dream that sleep o'er-power'd me

In midst of all this heaven ? Why not see,

Far off, the shadows of his pinions dark,

And stare them from me ? But no, like a spark

That needs must die, although its little beam

Reflects upon a diamond, my sweet dream

Fell into nothing—into stupid sleep.

And so it was, until a gentle creep,

A careful moving caught my waking ears,   680

And up I started Ah ' my sighs, my tears,

My clenched hands ,—for lo ' the poppies hung

Dew-dabbled on their stalks, the ouzel sung

A heavy ditty, and the sullen day

Had chidden herald Hesperus away,

With leaden looks the solitary breeze

Bluster'd, and slept, and its wild self did teaze

With wayward melancholy , and I thought,

Mark me, Peona ' that sometimes it brought

Faint fare-thee-wells, and sigh-shrilled adieus '—   690

Away I wander'd—all the pleasant hues

Of heaven and earth had faded deepest shades

Were deepest dungeons , heaths and sunny glades

Were full of pestilent light, our taintless rills

, Seem'd sooty, and o'er-spread with upturn'd gills

Of dying fish, the vermeil rose had blown

In frightful scarlet, and its thorns out-grown

Like spiked aloe   If an innocent bird

Before my heedless footsteps stirr'd, and stirr'd

In little journeys, I beheld in it   700

A disguis'd demon, missioned to knit

My soul with under darkness, to entice

My stumblings down some monstrous precipice

Therefore I eager followed, and did curse

The disappointment   Time, that aged nurse,

Rock'd me to patience   Now, thank gentle heaven!

These things, with all their comfortings, are given

To my down-sunken hours, and with thee,

Sweet sister, help to stem the ebbing sea

Of weary life "   710

         Thus ended he, and both

Sat silent · for the maid was very loth

To answer, feeling well that breathed words

Would all be lost, unheard, and vain as swords

Against the enchased crocodile, or leaps

Of grasshoppers against the sun   She weeps,

And wonders, struggles to devise some blame,

To put on such a look as would say, *Shame*

On this poor weakness! but, for all her strife,

She could as soon have crush'd away the life   720

From a sick dove   At length, to break the pause,

She said with trembling chance   " Is this the cause?

This all? Yet it is strange, and sad, alas !

That one who through this middle earth should pass

Most like a sojourning demi-god, and leave

His name upon the harp-string, should achieve

No higher bard than simple maidenhood,

Singing alone, and fearfully,—how the blood

Left his young cheek , and how he used to stray

He knew not where, and how he would say, *nay*,   730

If any said 'twas love   and yet 'twas love ,

What could it be but love ? How a ring-dove

Let fall a sprig of yew tree in his path ,

And how he died   and then, that love doth scathe,

The gentle heart, as northern blasts do roses ,

And then the ballad of his sad life closes

With sighs, and an alas '—Endymion '

Be rather in the trumpet's mouth,—anon

Among the winds at large—that all may hearken '

Although, before the crystal heavens darken,   740

I watch and dote upon the silver lakes

Pictur'd in western cloudiness, that takes

The semblance of gold rocks and bright gold sands,

Islands, and creeks, and amber-fretted strands

With horses prancing o'er them, palaces

And towers of amethyst,—would I so tease

My pleasant days, because I could not mount

Into those regions ? The Morphean fount

Of that fine element that visions, dreams,

And fitful whims of sleep are made of, streams   750

Into its airy channels with so subtle,

So thin a breathing, not the spider's shuttle,

Circled a million times within the space

Of a swallow's nest-door, could delay a trace,

A tinting of its quality   how light

Must dreams themselves be , seeing they're more slight

Than the mere nothing that engenders them '

Then wherefore sully the entrusted gem

Of high and noble life with thoughts so sick?

Why pierce high-fronted honour to the quick   760

For nothing but a dream?" Hereat the youth

Look'd up   a conflicting of shame and ruth

Was in his plaited brow   yet, his eyelids

Widened a little, as when Zephyr bids

A little breeze to creep between the fans

Of careless butterflies   amid his pains

He seem'd to taste a drop of manna-dew,

Full palatable , and a colour grew

Upon his cheek, while thus he lifeful spake.

" Peona ! ever have I long'd to slake   770

My thirst for the world's praises   nothing base,

No merely slumberous phantasm, could unlace

The stubborn canvas for my voyage prepar'd—

Though now 'tis tatter'd , leaving my bark bar'd

And sullenly drifting   yet my higher hope

Is of too wide, too rainbow-large a scope,

To fret at myriads of earthly wrecks

Wherein lies happiness ? In that which becks

Our ready minds to fellowship divine,

A fellowship with essence , till we shine,   780

Full alchemiz'd, and free of space.   Behold

The clear religion of heaven ' Fold

A rose leaf round thy finger's taperness,

And soothe thy lips   hist, when the airy stress

Of music's kiss impregnates the free winds,

And with a sympathetic touch unbinds

Eolian magic from their lucid wombs

Then old songs waken from enclouded tombs ,

Old ditties sigh above their father's grave,

Ghosts of melodious prophecyings rave   790

Round every spot were trod Apollo's foot ,

Bronze clarions awake, and faintly bruit,

Where long ago a giant battle was ,

And, from the turf, a lullaby doth pass

In every place where infant Orpheus slept.

Feel we these things ?—that moment have we stept

Into a sort of oneness, and our state

Is like a floating spirit's   But there are

Richer entanglements, enthralments far

More self-destroying, leading, by degrees,   800

To the chief intensity   the crown of these

Is made of love and friendship, and sits high
Upon the forehead of humanity
All its more ponderous and bulky worth
Is friendship, whence there ever issues forth
A steady splendour, but at the tip-top,
There hangs by unseen film, an orbed drop
Of light, and that is love its influence,
Thrown in our eyes, genders a novel sense,
At which we start and fret, till in the end,   810
Melting into its radiance, we blend,
Mingle, and so become a part of it,—
Nor with aught else can our souls interknit
So wingedly when we combine therewith,
Life's self is nourish'd by its proper pith,
And we are nurtured like a pelican brood
Aye, so delicious is the unsating food,
That men, who might have tower'd in the van
Of all the congregated world, to fan
And winnow from the coming step of time   820
All chaff of custom, wipe away all slime
Left by men-slugs and human serpentry,
Have been content to let occasion die,

Whilst they did sleep in love's elysium

And, truly, I would rather be struck dumb,

Than speak against this ardent listlessness

For I have ever thought that it might bless

The world with benefits unknowingly ,

As does the nightingale, upperched high,

And cloister'd among cool and bunched leaves—   830

She sings but to her love, nor e'er conceives

How tiptoe Night holds back her dark-grey hood

Just so may love, although 'tis understood

The mere commingling of passionate breath,

Produce more than our searching witnesseth .

What I know not   but who, of men, can tell

That flowers would bloom, or that green fruit would

       swell

To melting pulp, that fish would have bright mail,

The earth its dower of river, wood, and vale,

The meadows runnels, runnels pebble-stones,   840

The seed its harvest, or the lute its tones,

Tones ravishment, or ravishment its sweet,

If human souls did never kiss and greet?

" Now, if this earthly love has power to make

Men's being mortal, immortal, to shake

Ambition from their memories, and brim

Their measure of content, what merest whim,

Seems all this poor endeavour after fame,

To one, who keeps within his stedfast aim

A love immortal, an immortal too   850

Look not so wilder'd, for these things are true,

And never can be born of atomies

That buzz about our slumbers, like brain-flies,

Leaving us fancy-sick   No, no, I'm sure,

My restless spirit never could endure

To brood so long upon one luxury,

Unless it did, though fearfully, espy

A hope beyond the shadow of a dream.

My sayings will the less obscured seem,

When I have told thee how my waking sight   860

Has made me scruple whether that same night

Was pass'd in dreaming   Hearken, sweet Peona '

Beyond the matron-temple of Latona,

Which we should see but for these darkening boughs,

Lies a deep hollow, from whose ragged brows

Bushes and trees do lean all round athwart,

And meet so nearly, that with wings outraught,

And spreaded tail, a vulture could not glide

Past them, but he must brush on every side

Some moulder'd steps lead into this cool cell,   870

Far as the slabbed margin of a well,

Whose patient level peeps its crystal eye

Right upward, through the bushes, to the sky

Oft have I brought thee flowers, on their stalks set

Like vestal primroses, but dark velvet

Edges them round, and they have golden pits

'Twas there I got them, from the gaps and slits

In a mossy stone, that sometimes was my seat,

When all above was faint with mid-day heat

And there in strife no burning thoughts to heed,   880

I'd bubble up the water through a reed ,

So reaching back to boy-hood   make me ships

Of moulted feathers, touchwood, alder chips,

With leaves stuck in them , and the Neptune be

Of their petty ocean   Oftener, heavily,

When love-lorn hours had left me less a child,

I sat contemplating the figures wild

Of o'er-head clouds melting the mirror through
Upon a day, while thus I watch'd, by flew
A cloudy Cupid, with his bow and quiver,   890
So plainly character'd, no breeze would shiver
The happy chance   so happy, I was fain
To follow it upon the open plain,
And, therefore, was just going, when, behold!
A wonder, fair as any I have told—
The same bright face I tasted in my sleep,
Smiling in the clear well.   My heart did leap
Through the cool depth —It moved as if to flee—
I started up, when lo! refreshfully,
There came upon my face, in plenteous showers,   900
Dew-drops, and dewy buds, and leaves, and flowers,
Wrapping all objects from my smothered sight,
Bathing my spirit in a new delight
Aye, such a breathless honey-feel of bliss
Alone preserved me from the drear abyss
Of death, for the fair form had gone again
Pleasure is oft a visitant, but pain
Clings cruelly to us, like the gnawing sloth
On the deer's tender haunches   late, and loth,

'Tis scar'd away by slow returning pleasure   910
How sickening, how dark the dreadful leisure
Of weary days, made deeper exquisite,
By a fore-knowledge of unslumbrous night!
Like sorrow came upon me, heavier still,
Than when I wander'd from the poppy hill
And a whole age of lingering moments crept
Sluggishly by, ere more contentment swept
Away at once the deadly yellow spleen
Yes, thrice have I this fair enchantment seen,
Once more been tortured with renewed life   920
When last the wintry gusts gave over strife
With the conquering sun of spring, and left the skies
Warm and serene, but yet with moistened eyes
In pity of the shatter'd infant buds,—
That time thou didst adorn, with amber studs,
My hunting cap, because I laugh'd and smil'd,
Chatted with thee, and many days exil'd
All torment from my breast;—'twas even then,
Straying about, yet, coop'd up in the den
Of helpless discontent,—hurling my lance   930
From place to place, and following at chance,

At last, by hap, through some young trees it struck,

And, plashing among bedded pebbles, stuck

In the middle of a brook,—whose silver ramble

Down twenty little falls, through reeds and bramble,

Tracing along, it brought me to a cave,

Whence it ran brightly forth, and white did lave

The nether sides of mossy stones and rock,—

'Mong which it gurgled blythe adieus, to mock

Its own sweet grief at parting.   Overhead,   940

Hung a lush scene of drooping weeds, and spread

Thick, as to curtain up some wood-nymph's home.

" Ah ! impious mortal, whither do I roam ?"

Said I, low voic'd   " Ah, whither ! 'Tis the grot

Of Proserpine, when Hell, obscure and hot,

Doth her resign , and where her tender hands

She dabbles, on the cool and sluicy sands

Or 'tis the cell of Echo, where she sits,

And babbles thorough silence, till her wits

Are gone in tender madness, and anon,   950

Faints into sleep, with many a dying tone

Of sadness   O that she would take my vows,

And breathe them sighingly among the boughs,

To sue her gentle ears for whose fair head,

Daily, I pluck sweet flowerets from their bed,

And weave them dyingly—send honey-whispers

Round every leaf, that all those gentle lispers

May sigh my love unto her pitying !

O charitable echo ! hear, and sing

This ditty to her !—tell her"—so I stay'd   960

My foolish tongue, and listening, half afraid,

Stood stupefied with my own empty folly,

And blushing for the freaks of melancholy.

Salt tears were coming, when I heard my name

Most fondly lipp'd, and then these accents came

" Endymion ! the cave is secreter

Than the isle of Delos   Echo hence shall stir

No sighs but sigh-warm kisses, or light noise

Of thy combing hand, the while it travelling cloys

And trembles through my labyrinthine hair "   970

At that oppress'd I hurried in—Ah ! where

Are those swift moments? Whither are they fled?

I'll smile no more, Peona, nor will wed

Sorrow the way to death, but patiently

Bear up against it   so farewel, sad sigh,

And come instead demurest meditation,
To occupy me wholly, and to fashion
My pilgrimage for the world's dusky brink.
No more will I count over, link by link,
My chain of grief   no longer strive to find   980
A half-forgetfulness in mountain wind
Blustering about my ears   aye, thou shalt see,
Dearest of sisters, what my life shall be ,
What a calm round of hours shall make my days
There is a paly flame of hope that plays
Where'er I look   but yet, I'll say 'tis naught—
And here I bid it die   Have not I caught,
Already, a more healthy countenance?
By this the sun is setting , we may chance
Meet some of our near-dwellers with my car "   990

     This said, he rose, faint-smiling like a star
Through autumn mists, and took Peona's hand
They stept into the boat, and launch'd from land

ENDYMION

BOOK II

ENDYMION.

BOOK II

O sovereign power of love! O grief! O balm!
All records, saving thine, come cool, and calm,
And shadowy, through the mist of passed years
For others, good or bad, hatred and tears
Have become indolent, but touching thine,
One sigh doth echo, one poor sob doth pine,
One kiss brings honey-dew from buried days
The woes of Troy, towers smothering o'er their blaze,
Stiff-holden shields, far-piercing spears, keen blades,
Struggling, and blood, and shrieks—all dimly fades   10

Into some backward corner of the brain,

Yet, in our very souls, we feel amain

The close of Troilus and Cressid sweet

Hence, pageant history! hence, gilded cheat!

Swart planet in the universe of deeds!

Wide sea, that one continuous murmur breeds

Along the pebbled shore of memory!

Many old rotten-timber'd boats there be

Upon thy vaporous bosom, magnified

To goodly vessels, many a sail of pride,   20

And golden keel'd, is left unlaunch'd and dry

But wherefore this? What care, though owl did fly

About the great Athenian admiral's mast?

What care, though striding Alexander past

The Indus with his Macedonian numbers?

Though old Ulysses tortured from his slumbers

The glutted Cyclops, what care?—Juliet leaning

Amid her window-flowers,—sighing,—weaning

Tenderly her fancy from its maiden snow,

Doth more avail than these   the silver flow   30

Of Hero's tears, the swoon of Imogen,

Fair Pastorella in the bandit's den,

Are things to brood on with more ardency
Than the death-day of empires   Fearfully
Must such conviction come upon his head,
Who, thus far, discontent, has dared to tread,
Without one muse's smile, or kind behest,
The path of love and poesy   But rest,
In chaffing restlessness, is yet more drear
Than to be rush'd, in striving to uprear   40
Love's standard on the battlements of song
So once more days and nights aid me along,
Like legion'd soldiers

               Brain-sick shepherd prince,
What promise hast thou faithful guarded since
The day of sacrifice? Or, have new sorrows
Come with the constant dawn upon thy morrows?
Alas ! 'tis his old grief   For many days,
Has he been wandering in uncertain ways
Through wilderness, and woods of mossed oaks ,   50
Counting his woe-worn minutes, by the strokes
Of the lone woodcutter , and listening still,
Hour after hour, to each lush-leav'd rill.

Now he is sitting by a shady spring,

And elbow-deep with feverous fingering

Stems the upbursting cold   a wild rose tree

Pavilions him in bloom, and he doth see

A bud which snares his fancy   lo ! but now

He plucks it, dips its stalk in the water   how !

It swells, it buds, it flowers beneath his sight,   60

And, in the middle, there is softly pight

A golden butterfly , upon whose wings

There must be surely character'd strange things,

For with wide eye he wonders, and smiles oft

 Lightly this little herald flew aloft,

Follow'd by glad Endymion's clasped hands

Onward it flies   From languor's sullen bands

His limbs are loos'd, and eager, on he hies

Dazzled to trace it in the sunny skies

It seem'd he flew, the way so easy was ,   70

And like a new-born spirit did he pass

Through the green evening quiet in the sun,

O'er many a heath, through many a woodland dun,

Through buried paths, where sleepy twilight dreams

The summer time away   One track unseams

A wooded cleft, and, far away, the blue

Of ocean fades upon him, then, anew,

He sinks adown a solitary glen,

Where there was never sound of mortal men,

Saving, perhaps, some snow-light cadences   80

Melting to silence, when upon the breeze

Some holy bark let forth an anthem sweet,

To cheer itself to Delphi   Still his feet

Went swift beneath the merry-winged guide,

Until it reached a splashing fountain's side

That, near a cavern's mouth, for ever pour'd

Unto the temperate air   then high it soar'd,

And, downward, suddenly began to dip,

As if, athirst with so much toil, 'twould sip

The crystal spout-head   so it did, with touch   90

Most delicate, as though afraid to smutch

Even with mealy gold the waters clear

But, at that very touch, to disappear

So fairy-quick, was strange !   Bewildered,

Endymion sought around, and shook each bed

Of covert flowers in vain, and then he flung

Himself along the grass   What gentle tongue,

What whisperer disturb'd his gloomy rest?

It was a nymph uprisen to the breast

In the fountain's pebbly margin, and she stood   100

'Mong lilies, like the youngest of the brood

To him her dripping hand she softly kist,

And anxiously began to plait and twist

Her ringlets round her fingers, saying   " Youth '

Too long, alas, hast thou starv'd on the ruth,

The bitterness of love   too long indeed,

Seeing thou art so gentle   Could I weed

Thy soul of care, by heavens, I would offer

All the bright riches of my crystal coffer

To Amphitrite, all my clear-eyed fish,   110

Golden, or rainbow-sided, or purplish,

Vermilion-tail'd, or finn'd with silvery gauze,

Yea, or my veined pebble-floor, that draws

A virgin light to the deep, my grotto-sands

Tawny and gold, ooz'd slowly from far lands

By my diligent springs, my level lilies, shells,

My charming rod, my potent river spells,

Yes, every thing, even to the pearly cup

Meander gave me,—for I bubbled up

To fainting creatures in a desert wild   120

But woe is me, I am but as a child

To gladden thee , and all I dare to say,

Is, that I pity thee , that on this day

I've been thy guide, that thou must wander far

In other regions, past the scanty bar

To mortal steps, before thou cans't be ta'en

From every wasting sigh, from every pain,

Into the gentle bosom of thy love

Why it is thus, one knows in heaven above

But, a poor Naiad, I guess not   Farewel !   130

I have a ditty for my hollow cell "

    Hereat, she vanished from Endymion's gaze,

Who brooded o'er the water in amaze

The dashing fount pour'd on, and where its pool

Lay, half asleep, in grass and rushes cool,

Quick waterflies and gnats were sporting still,

And fish were dimpling, as if good nor ill

Had fallen out that hour   The wanderer,

Holding his forehead, to keep off the burr

Of smothering fancies, patiently sat down ,   140

And, while beneath the evening's sleepy frown

Glow-worms began to trim their starry lamps,

Thus breath'd he to himself " Whoso encamps

To take a fancied city of delight,

O what a wretch is he ! and when 'tis his,

After long toil and travelling, to miss

The kernel of his hopes, how more than vile

Yet, for him there's refreshment even in toil ,

Another city doth he set about,

Free from the smallest pebble-head of doubt   150

That he will seize on trickling honey-combs

Alas, he finds them dry, and then he foams,

And onward to another city speeds

But this is human life   the war, the deeds,

The disappointment, the anxiety,

Imagination's struggles, far and nigh,

All human , bearing in themselves this good,

That they are still the air, the subtle food,

To make us feel existence, and to shew

How quiet death is   Where soil is men grow,   160

Whether to weeds or flowers, but for me,

There is no depth to strike in   I can see

Nought earthly worth my compassing, so stand

Upon a misty, jutting head of land—

Alone? No, no, and by the Orphean lute,

When mad Eurydice is listening to't,

I'd rather stand upon this misty peak,

With not a thing to sigh for, or to seek,

But the soft shadow of my thrice-seen love,

Than be—I care not what   O meekest dove   170

Of heaven! O Cynthia, ten-times bright and fair!

From thy blue throne, now filling all the air,

Glance but one little beam of temper'd light

Into my bosom, that the dreadful might

And tyranny of love be somewhat scar'd!

Yet do not so, sweet queen, one torment spar'd,

Would give a pang to jealous misery,

Worse than the torment's self   but rather tie

Large wings upon my shoulders, and point out

My love's far dwelling   Though the playful rout   180

Of Cupids shun thee, too divine art thou,

Too keen in beauty, for thy silver prow

Not to have dipp'd in love's most gentle stream

O be propitious, nor severely deem

My madness impious , for, by all the stars

That tend thy bidding, I do think the bars

That kept my spirit in are burst—that I

Am sailing with thee through the dizzy sky !

How beautiful thou art ! The world how deep !

How tremulous-dazzlingly the wheels sweep   190

Around their axle ! Then these gleaming reins,

How lithe ! When this thy chariot attains

Its airy goal, haply some bower veils

Those twilight eyes ? Those eyes !—my spirit fails—

Dear goddess, help ! or the wide-gaping air

Will gulph me—help !"—At this with madden'd stare,

And lifted hands, and trembling lips he stood ,

Like old Deucalion mountain'd o'er the flood,

Or blind Orion hungry for the morn

And, but from the deep cavern there was borne   200

A voice, he had been froze to senseless stone ,

Nor sigh of his, nor plaint, nor passion'd moan

Had more been heard. Thus swell'd it forth " Descend,

Young mountaineer ! descend where alleys bend

Into the sparry hollows of the world!
Oft hast thou seen bolts of the thunder hurl'd
As from thy threshold, day by day hast been
A little lower than the chilly sheen
Of icy pinnacles, and dipp'dst thine arms
Into the deadening ether that still charms   210
Their marble being. now, as deep profound
As those are high, descend! He ne'er is crown'd
With immortality, who fears to follow
Where airy voices lead   so through the hollow,
The silent mysteries of earth, descend!"

He heard but the last words, nor could contend
One moment in reflection   for he fled
Into the fearful deep, to hide his head
From the clear moon, the trees, and coming madness

'Twas far too strange, and wonderful for sadness,
Sharpening, by degrees, his appetite   221
To dive into the deepest   Dark, nor light,
The region, nor bright, nor sombre wholly,
But mingled up, a gleaming melancholy,

A dusky empire and its diadems,

One faint eternal eventide of gems

Aye, millions sparkled on a vein of gold,

Along whose track the prince quick footsteps told,

With all its lines abrupt and angular

Out-shooting sometimes, like a meteor-star,   230

Through a vast antre, then the metal woof,

Like Vulcan's rainbow, with some monstrous roof

Curves hugely now, far in the deep abyss,

It seems an angry lightning, and doth hiss

Fancy into belief anon it leads

Through winding passages, where sameness breeds

Vexing conceptions of some sudden change,

Whether to silver grots, or giant range

Of sapphire columns, or fantastic bridge

Athwart a flood of crystal. On a ridge   240

Now fareth he, that o'er the vast beneath

Towers like an ocean-cliff, and whence he seeth

A hundred waterfalls, whose voices come

But as the murmuring surge. Chilly and numb

His bosom grew, when first he, far away,

Descried an orbed diamond, set to fray

Old darkness from his throne   'twas like the sun

Uprisen o'er chaos   and with such a stun

Came the amazement, that, absorb'd in it,

He saw not fiercer wonders—past the wit   250

Of any spirit to tell, but one of those

Who, when this planet's sphering time doth close,

Will be its high remembrancers   who they?

The mighty ones who have made eternal day

For Greece and England   While astonishment

With deep-drawn sighs was quieting, he went

Into a marble gallery, passing through

A mimic temple, so complete and true

In sacred custom, that he well nigh fear'd

To search it inwards, whence far off appear'd,   260

Through a long pillar'd vista, a fair shrine,

And, just beyond, on light tiptoe divine,

A quiver'd Dian   Stepping awfully,

The youth approach'd, oft turning his veil'd eye

Down sidelong aisles, and into niches old

And when, more near against the marble cold

He had touch'd his forehead, he began to thread

All courts and passages, where silence dead

F

Rous'd by his whispering footsteps murmured faint

And long he travers'd to and fro, to acquaint   270

Himself with every mystery, and awe ,

Till, weary, he sat down before the maw

Of a wide outlet, fathomless and dim

To wild uncertainty and shadows grim.

There, when new wonders ceas'd to float before,

And thoughts of self came on, how crude and sore

The journey homeward to habitual self !

A mad-pursuing of the fog-born elf,

Whose flitting lantern, through rude nettle-briar,

Cheats us into a swamp, into a fire,   280

Into the bosom of a hated thing

What misery most drowningly doth sing

In lone Endymion's ear, now he has caught

The goal of consciousness ?   Ah, 'tis the thought,

The deadly feel of solitude   for lo !

He cannot see the heavens, nor the flow

Of rivers, nor hill-flowers running wild

In pink and purple chequer, nor, up-pil'd,

The cloudy rack slow journeying in the west,

Like herded elephants, nor felt, nor prest   290

Cool grass, nor tasted the fresh slumberous air,

But far from such companionship to wear

An unknown time, surcharg'd with grief, away,

Was now his lot   And must he patient stay,

Tracing fantastic figures with his spear?

" No!" exclaimed he, " why should I tarry here?"

No! loudly echoed times innumerable

At which he straightway started, and 'gan tell

His paces back into the temple's chief,

Warming and glowing strong in the belief   300

Of help from Dian   so that when again

He caught her airy form, thus did he plain,

Moving more near the while   " O Haunter chaste

Of river sides, and woods, and heathy waste,

Where with thy silver bow and arrows keen

Art thou now forested? O woodland Queen,

What smoothest air thy smoother forehead woos?

Where dost thou listen to the wide halloos

Of thy disparted nymphs? Through what dark tree

Glimmers thy crescent? Wheresoe'er it be,   310

'Tis in the breath of heaven   thou dost taste

Freedom as none can taste it, nor dost waste

Thy loveliness in dismal elements,

But, finding in our green earth sweet contents,

There livest blissfully　　Ah, if to thee

It feels Elysian, how rich to me,

An exil'd mortal, sounds its pleasant name !

Within my breast there lives a choking flame—

O let me cool it among the zephyr-boughs !

A homeward fever parches up my tongue—　　　　320

O let me slake it at the running springs !

Upon my ear a noisy nothing rings—

O let me once more hear the linnet's note !

Before mine eyes thick films and shadows float—

O let me 'noint them with the heaven's light !

Dost thou now lave thy feet and ankles white ?

O think how sweet to me the freshening sluice !

Dost thou now please thy thirst with berry-juice ?

O think how this dry palate would rejoice !

If in soft slumber thou dost hear my voice,　　　　330

O think how I should love a bed of flowers !—

Young goddess ! let me see my native bowers !

Deliver me from this rapacious deep !"

Thus ending loudly, as he would o'erleap
His destiny, alert he stood but when
Obstinate silence came heavily again,
Feeling about for its old couch of space
And airy cradle, lowly bow'd his face
Desponding, o'er the marble floor's cold thrill
But 'twas not long, for, sweeter than the rill   340
To its old channel, or a swollen tioe
To margin sallows, were the leaves he spied,
And flowers, and wreaths, and ready myrtle crowns
Up heaping through the slab refreshment drowns
Itself, and strives its own delights to hide—
Nor in one spot alone, the floral pride
In a long whispering birth enchanted grew
Before his footsteps, as when heav'd anew
Old ocean rolls a lengthened wave to the shore,
Down whose green back the short-liv'd foam, all hoar,
Bursts gradual, with a wayward indolence   351

Increasing still in heart, and pleasant sense,
Upon his fairy journey on he hastes,

So anxious for the end, he scarcely wastes
One moment with his hand among the sweets
Onward he goes—he stops—his bosom beats
As plainly in his ear, as the faint charm
Of which the throbs were born   This still alarm,
This sleepy music, forc'd him walk tiptoe
For it came more softly than the east could blow   360
Arion's magic to the Atlantic isles,
Or than the west, made jealous by the smiles
Of thron'd Apollo, could breathe back the lyre
To seas Ionian and Tyrian

    O did he ever live, that lonely man,
Who lov'd—and music slew not? 'Tis the pest
Of love, that fairest joys give most unrest,
That things of delicate and tenderest worth
Are swallow'd all, and made a seared dearth,
By one consuming flame   it doth immerse   370
And suffocate true blessings in a curse
Half-happy, by comparison of bliss,
Is miserable   'Twas even so with this

Dew-dropping melody, in the Carian's ear,
First heaven, then hell, and then forgotten clear,
Vanish'd in elemental passion

And down some swart abysm he had gone,
Had not a heavenly guide benignant led
To where thick myrtle branches, 'gainst his head
Brushing, awakened   then the sounds again   380
Went noiseless as a passing noontide rain
Over a bower, where little space he stood,
For as the sunset peeps into a wood
So saw he panting light, and towards it went
Through winding alleys, and lo, wonderment!
Upon soft verdure saw, one here, one there,
Cupids a slumbering on their pinions fair

After a thousand mazes overgone,
At last, with sudden step, he came upon
A chamber, myrtle wall'd, embowered high,   390
Full of light, incense, tender minstrelsy,
And more of beautiful and strange beside
For on a silken couch of rosy pride,

In midst of all, there lay a sleeping youth
Of fondest beauty, fonder, in fair sooth,
Than sighs could fathom, or contentment reach
And coverlids gold-tinted like the peach,
Or ripe October's faded marigolds,
Fell sleek about him in a thousand folds—
Not hiding up an Apollonian curve   400
Of neck and shoulder, nor the tenting swerve
Of knee from knee, nor ankles pointing light,
But rather, giving them to the filled sight
Officiously   Sideway his face repos'd
On one white arm, and tenderly unclos'd,
By tenderest pressure, a faint damask mouth
To slumbery pout, just as the morning south
Disparts a dew-lipp'd rose   Above his head,
Four lily stalks did their white honours wed
To make a coronal, and round him grew   410
All tendrils green, of every bloom and hue,
Together intertwin'd and trammel'd fresh
The vine of glossy sprout, the ivy mesh,
Shading its Ethiop berries, and woodbine,
Of velvet leaves and bugle-blooms divine,

Convolvulus in streaked vases flush ,
The creeper, mellowing for an autumn blush ,
And virgin's bower, trailing airily ,
With others of the sisterhood   Hard by,
Stood serene Cupids watching silently   420
One, kneeling to a lyre, touch'd the strings,
Muffling to death the pathos with his wings ,
And, ever and anon, uprose to look
At the youth's slumber , while another took
A willow-bough, distilling odorous dew,
And shook it on his hair , another flew
In through the woven roof, and fluttering-wise
Rain'd violets upon his sleeping eyes

     At these enchantments, and yet many more,
The breathless Latmian wonder'd o'er and o'er ,   430
Until, impatient in embarrassment,
He forthright pass'd, and lightly treading went
To that same feather'd lyrist, who straightway,
Smiling, thus whisper'd   " Though from upper day
Thou art a wanderer, and thy presence here
Might seem unholy, be of happy cheer !

For 'tis the nicest touch of human honour,

When some ethereal and high-favouring donor

Presents immortal bowers to mortal sense,

As now 'tis done to thee, Endymion   Hence   140

Was I in no wise startled   So recline

Upon these living flowers   Here is wine,

Alive with sparkles—never, I aver,

Since Ariadne was a vintager,

So cool a purple   taste these juicy pears,

Sent me by sad Vertumnus, when his fears

Were high about Pomona   here is cream,

Deepening to richness from a snowy gleam,

Sweeter than that nurse Amalthea skimm'd

For the boy Jupiter   and here, undimm'd   150

By any touch, a bunch of blooming plums

Ready to melt between an infant's gums

And here is manna pick'd from Syrian trees,

In starlight, by the three Hesperides

Feast on, and meanwhile I will let thee know

Of all these things around us "   He did so,

Still brooding o'er the cadence of his lyre,

And thus   " I need not any hearing tire

By telling how the sea-born goddess pin'd
For a mortal youth, and how she strove to bind   460
Him all in all unto her doting self
Who would not be so prison'd? but, fond elf,
He was content to let her amorous plea
Faint through his careless arms, content to see
An unseiz'd heaven dying at his feet,
Content, O fool! to make a cold retreat,
When on the pleasant grass such love, lovelorn,
Lay sorrowing, when every tear was born
Of diverse passion, when her lips and eyes
Were clos'd in sullen moisture, and quick sighs   470
Came vex'd and pettish through her nostrils small
Hush! no exclaim—yet, justly mightst thou call
Curses upon his head —I was half glad,
But my poor mistress went distract and mad,
When the boar tusk'd him   so away she flew
To Jove's high throne, and by her plainings drew
Immortal tear-drops down the thunderer's beard,
Whereon, it was decreed he should be rear'd
Each summer time to life   Lo! this is he,
That same Adonis, safe in the privacy   480

Of this still region all his winter-sleep

Aye, sleep, for when our love-sick queen did weep

Over his waned corse, the tremulous shower

Heal'd up the wound, and, with a balmy power,

Medicined death to a lengthened drowsiness

The which she fills with visions, and doth dress

In all this quiet luxury, and hath set

Us young immortals, without any let,

To watch his slumber through   'Tis well nigh pass'd,

Even to a moment's filling up, and fast   490

She scuds with summer breezes, to pant through

The first long kiss, warm firstling, to renew

Embower'd sports in Cytherea's isle

Look ! how those winged listeners all this while

Stand anxious   see ! behold !"—This clamant word

Broke through the careful silence , for they heard

A rustling noise of leaves, and out there flutter'd

Pigeons and doves   Adonis something mutter'd,

The while one hand, that erst upon his thigh

Lay dormant, mov'd convuls'd and gradually   500

Up to his forehead   Then there was a hum

Of sudden voices, echoing, " Come ! come !

Arise ! awake ! Clear summer has forth walk'd

Unto the clover-sward, and she has talk'd

Full soothingly to every nested finch

Rise, Cupids ! or we'll give the blue-bell pinch

To your dimpled arms   Once more sweet life begin !"

At this, from every side they hurried in,

Rubbing their sleepy eyes with lazy wrists,

And doubling over head their little fists   510

In backward yawns   But all were soon alive

For as delicious wine doth, sparkling, dive

In nectar'd clouds and curls through water fair,

So from the arbour roof down swell'd an air

Odorous and enlivening , making all

To laugh, and play, and sing, and loudly call

For their sweet queen   when lo ! the wreathed green

Disparted, and far upward could be seen

Blue heaven, and a silver car, air-borne,

Whose silent wheels, fresh wet from clouds of morn,

Spun off a drizzling dew,—which falling chill   521

On soft Adonis' shoulders, made him still

Nestle and turn uneasily about

Soon were the white doves plain, with necks stretch'd out,

And silken traces lighten'd in descent,
And soon, returning from love's banishment,
Queen Venus leaning downward open arm'd
Her shadow fell upon his breast, and charm'd
A tumult to his heart, and a new life
Into his eyes   Ah, miserable strife,   530
But for her comforting ! unhappy sight,
But meeting her blue orbs ! Who, who can write
Of these first minutes ? The unchariest muse
To embracements warm as theirs makes coy excuse

O it has ruffled every spirit there,
Saving love's self, who stands superb to share
The general gladness   awfully he stands,
A sovereign quell is in his waving hands .
No sight can bear the lightning of his bow,
His quiver is mysterious, none can know   540
What themselves think of it, from forth his eyes
There darts strange light of varied hues and dyes
A scowl is sometimes on his brow, but who
Look full upon it feel anon the blue
Of his fair eyes run liquid through their souls

Endymion feels it, and no more controls
The burning prayer within him , so, bent low,
He had begun a plaining of his woe
But Venus, bending forward, said " My child,
Favour this gentle youth , his days are wild   550
With love—he—but alas ! too well I see
Thou know'st the deepness of his misery
Ah, smile not so, my son I tell thee true,
That when through heavy hours I used to rue
The endless sleep of this new-born Adon
This stranger ay I pitied For upon
A dreary morning once I fled away
Into the breezy clouds, to weep and pray
For this my love for vexing Mars had teaz'd
Me even to tears thence, when a little eas'd,   560
Down-looking, vacant, through a hazy wood,
I saw this youth as he despairing stood
Those same dark curls blown vagrant in the wind ,
Those same full fringed lids a constant blind
Over his sullen eyes I saw him throw
Himself on wither'd leaves, even as though
Death had come sudden , for no jot he mov'd,

Yet mutter'd wildly   I could hear he lov'd

Some fair immortal, and that his embrace

Had zoned her through the night   There is no trace 570

Of this in heaven   I have mark'd each cheek,

And find it is the vainest thing to seek ,

And that of all things 'tis kept secretest

Endymion ¹ one day thou wilt be blest

So still obey the guiding hand that fends

Thee safely through these wonders for sweet ends

'Tis a concealment needful in extreme ,

And if I guess'd not so, the sunny beam

Thou shouldst mount up to with me   Now adieu ¹

Here must we leave thee "—At these words up flew 580

The impatient doves, up rose the floating car,

Up went the hum celestial   High afar

The Latmian saw them minish into nought ,

And, when all were clear vanish'd, still he caught

A vivid lightning from that dreadful bow

When all was darkened, with Etnean throe

The earth clos'd—gave a solitary moan—

And left him once again in twilight lone

He did not rave, he did not stare aghast,

For all those visions were o'ergone, and past,   590

And he in loneliness   he felt assur'd

Of happy times, when all he had endur'd

Would seem a feather to the mighty prize

So, with unusual gladness, on he hies

Through caves, and palaces of mottled ore,

Gold dome, and crystal wall, and turquois floor,

Black polish'd porticos of awful shade,

And, at the last, a diamond balustrade,

Leading afar past wild magnificence,

Spiral through ruggedest loopholes, and thence   600

Stretching across a void, then guiding o'er

Enormous chasms, where, all foam and roar,

Streams subterranean tease their granite beds ,

Then heighten d just above the silvery heads

Of a thousand fountains, so that he could dash

The waters with his spear , but at the splash,

Done heedlessly, those spouting columns rose

Sudden a poplar's height, and 'gan to enclose

His diamond path with fretwork, streaming round

Alive, and dazzling cool, and with a sound,   610

G

Haply, like dolphin tumults, when sweet shells
Welcome the float of Thetis.   Long he dwells
On this delight , for, every minute's space,
The streams with changed magic interlace
Sometimes like delicatest lattices,
Cover'd with crystal vines , then weeping trees,
Moving about as in a gentle wind,
Which, in a wink, to watery gauze refin'd,
Pour'd into shapes of curtain'd canopies,
Spangled, and rich with liquid broideries   620
Of flowers, peacocks, swans, and naiads fair
Swifter than lightning went these wonders rare ,
And then the water, into stubborn streams
Collecting, mimick'd the wrought oaken beams,
Pillars, and frieze, and high fantastic roof,
Of those dusk places in times far aloof
Cathedrals call'd   He bade a loth farewel
To these founts Protean, passing gulph, and dell,
And torrent, and ten thousand jutting shapes,
Half seen through deepest gloom, and griesly gapes, 630
Blackening on every side, and overhead
A vaulted dome like Heaven's, far bespread

With starlight gems   aye, all so huge and strange,

The solitary felt a hurried change

Working within him into something dreary,—

Vex'd like a morning eagle, lost, and weary,

And purblind amid foggy, midnight wolds

But he revives at once   for who beholds

New sudden things, nor casts his mental slough?

Forth from a rugged arch, in the dusk below,   640

Came mother Cybele ! alone— alone—

In sombre chariot, dark foldings thrown

About her majesty, and front death-pale,

With turrets crown'd   Four maned lions hale

The sluggish wheels, solemn their toothed maws,

Their surly eyes brow-hidden, heavy paws

Uplifted drowsily, and nervy tails

Cowering their tawny brushes   Silent sails

This shadowy queen athwart, and faints away

In another gloomy arch   650

Wherefore delay,

Young traveller, in such a mournful place ?

Art thou wayworn, or canst not further trace

Lightning Source UK Ltd.
Milton Keynes UK
UKHW022317060922
408450UK00003B/33